TABLE OF CONTENTS

Introduction – Tell Me

Chapter 1 – Internet History

Chapter 2 - Computer vs. Internet Forensics

Chapter 3 - Useful tools for the "Amateur Internet Investigating Sleuth"

Chapter 4 - Online Resources

Chapter 5 - I Have a Special Gift for My Readers

Meet the Author

You Can Run but You Can't Hide
How to Become an Amateur Internet Sleuth
©Copyright 2012 by Dr. Leland Benton

Introduction – Tell Me

Dr. Leland Benton

"Tell me; where is cyberspace? Point out to me exactly where it is.

Show me the billion of airwaves coursing through our bodies and surroundings non-stop 24/7.

You have a website? Reach out and touch it for me.

Reach out and pluck a fax from the air. Or reach out and pluck the photo of your kid that you just sent grandma out of the air and show it to me.

Where is the Internet? And where are the billions of bits of information sent at seemingly light speed around the world. Show them to me.

The text message you sent…where did it go and how did it get there?

Show me the software you just downloaded and installed on your computer. Not the interface that pops up on your computer screen but show me the bits and bytes that make it work.

It is all AIR!!! It is nothing more than air. Every day we all buy, send and use air and every day we all do not realize that our lives are changing as new technology is released and as becomes a major part of our lives."

So begins my book "Selling Air" http://www.amazon.com/dp/B006JOIS5K. Scientists tell us that air is good for us and it is! We cannot live without air. But "air" can also be harmful to us and this "harmful air" is what this book is all about.

The Internet is a fantastic medium and worldwide community connection but inherent evil lurks in the background where you cannot see it. Evil people look for every opportunity to wreak havoc on your business as well as your person. Everything from spying on your cell phone to network intrusion and hacking…the bad guys are out there and patiently waiting to ensnare another victim.

The Internet provides a global network of communication and also a venue for deceptive marketing and advertising. From advertisers selling you cheap Viagra, to scammers promising you Nigerian Money Offers, to being announced the monthly winner of a foreign Lottery Club; you may wonder if anybody is out there going after the perpetrators of these scams. The short answer: YES, there is!

Here is just a partial list of things to watch for:

- **Online Auctions:** Misrepresented or undelivered goods
- **General Merchandise:** Misrepresented or undelivered goods not purchased through auctions
- **Fake Check Scams:** Consumers used fake checks to pay for sold items, and asked to have the money wired back
- **Nigerian Money Offers:** Deceptive promises of large sums of money, if consumers agreed to pay the transfer fee
- **Lotteries:** Asking winners to pay before claiming their non-existent prize
- **Advance Fee Loans:** Request a fee from consumers in exchange of promised personal loans
- **Phishing:** Emails pretending to represent a credible source, ask consumers for their personal information (e.g. credit card number)
- **Prizes/Sweepstakes:** Request a payment from consumers in order for them to claim their non-existent prize
- **Internet Access Services:** Misrepresentation of the cost of Internet access and other services, which are often not provided
- **Investments:** False promises of gains on investment

My quote above - *"You don't know how good the good news is until you first know how bad the bad news was!"* – is appropriate. I will first show you how bad the Internet is and then demonstrate to you just how easy it is to protect yourself and your family from the cyber den of thieves. Are you ready? Then let's get at it now...

And you think you have problems?

Chapter 1 – Internet History

Let's begin at the beginning. Many of my readers have no idea how and when the Internet came into being. I began on the Internet when it became available to the general public in 1989 and immediately saw the immense opportunity it offered. But at the same time, dirt bags from all over the world saw the same opportunity to deceive naïve people and as I learned all about the Internet and computers...they did too! So, from the beginning, the battle lines were drawn. And the war is brisk!

Email

E-mail predates the inception of the Internet, and was in fact a crucial tool in creating the Internet. MIT first demonstrated the Compatible Time-Sharing System (CTSS) in 1961. It allowed multiple users to log into the IBM 7094 from remote dial-up terminals, and to store files online on disk. This new ability encouraged users to share information in new ways.

E-mail started in 1965 as a way for multiple users of a time-sharing mainframe computer to communicate. The ARPANET computer network made a large contribution to the development of e-mail.

There is one report that indicates experimental inter-system e-mail transfers began shortly after its creation in 1969. Ray Tomlinson initiated the use of the "@ sign" to separate the names of the user and their machine in 1971. The ARPANET significantly increased the popularity of e-mail, and it became the killer app of the ARPANET.

Internet

The **Internet** is a global system of interconnected computer networks that interchange data by packet switching using the standardized Internet Protocol Suite (TCP/IP). It is a "network of networks" that consists of millions of private and public, academic, business, and government networks of local to global scope. The Internet carries various information resources and services, such as electronic mail, online chat, file transfer and file sharing, online gaming, and the inter-linked hypertext documents and other resources of the World Wide Web (WWW).

A 1946 comic science-fiction story, A Logic Named Joe, by Murray Leinster laid out the Internet and many of its strengths and weaknesses. However, it took more than a decade before reality began to catch up with this vision. The USSR's launch of Sputnik spurred the United States to create the Advanced Research Projects Agency, known as ARPA, in February 1958 to regain a technological lead.

The first two nodes of what would become the ARPANET were interconnected between UCLA and SRI International in Menlo Park, California, on October 29, 1969. Use of the term "Internet" to describe a single global TCP/IP network originated in December 1974. During the next nine years, work proceeded to refine the protocols and to implement them on a wide range of operating systems.

The first TCP/IP-based wide-area network was operational by January 1, 1983 when all hosts on the ARPANET were switched over from the older NCP protocols. In 1985, the United States' National Science Foundation (NSF) commissioned the construction of the NSFNET

The opening of the network to commercial interests began in 1988. The US Federal Networking Council approved the interconnection of the NSFNET to the commercial MCI Mail system in that year and the link was made in the summer of 1989.

Other commercial electronic e-mail services were soon connected. In that same year, the first three commercial Internet service providers (ISP) were created; important, separate networks that offered gateways into, and then later merged with, the Internet.

Various other commercial and educational networks were interconnected with the growing Internet. Telenet (later called Sprintnet) was a large privately funded national computer network with free dial-up access in cities throughout the U.S. that had been in operation since the 1970s. This network was eventually interconnected with the others in the 1980s as the TCP/IP protocol became increasingly popular.

The ability of TCP/IP to work over virtually any pre-existing communication networks allowed for a great ease of growth, although the rapid growth of the Internet was due primarily to the availability of commercial routers, the availability of commercial Ethernet equipment for local-area networking and the widespread implementation of TCP/IP on the UNIX operating system.

Growth

Although the basic applications and guidelines that make the Internet possible had existed for almost a decade, the network did not gain a truly public face until the August 6, 1991. The World Wide Web was invented by English scientist Tim Berners-Lee in 1989.

On 25 December 1990 he implemented the first successful communication between an HTTP client and server via the Internet. Berners-Lee is the director of the World Wide Web Consortium (W3C), which oversees the Web's continued development.

An early popular web browser was ViolaWWW, patterned after HyperCard and built using the X Window System. It was eventually replaced in popularity by the Mosaic web browser. In 1993, the National Center for Supercomputing Applications at the University of Illinois released version 1.0 of Mosaic, and by late 1994 there was growing public interest in the previously academic, technical Internet.

By 1996 usage of the word *Internet* had become commonplace, and consequently, so had World Wide Web. Meanwhile, over the course of the decade, the Internet successfully accommodated the majority of previously existing public computer networks.

During the 1990s, it was estimated that the Internet grew by 100% per year, with a brief period of explosive growth in 1996 and 1997.

Chapter 2 - Computer vs. Internet Forensics

The widespread use of computer forensics resulted from the convergence of two factors: the increasing dependence of law enforcement on computing (as in the area of fingerprints) and the ubiquity of computers that followed from the microcomputer revolution. As computer forensics evolved, it was modeled after the basic investigative methodologies of law enforcement and the security industry that championed its use. Not surprisingly, computer forensics is about the "preservation, identification, extraction, documentation and interpretation of computer data." In order to accomplish these goals, there are well-defined procedures, also derived from law enforcement, for acquiring and analyzing the evidence without damaging it and authenticating the evidence and providing a chain-of-custody that will hold up in court. The tools for the "search-and-seizure" side of computer forensics are a potpourri of sophisticated tools that are primarily focused on the physical side of computing: i.e., tracing and locating computer hardware, recovering hidden data from storage media, identifying and recovering hidden data, decrypting files, decompressing data, cracking passwords, "crowbarring" an operating system (bypassing normal security controls and permissions), and so forth. For those who are old enough to remember the original Norton Utilities for DOS think of these modern tools as the original Norton Disk Editor for DOS on steroids.

Some noteworthy observations:

(1) HelpAssistant, and "Support" accounts and passwords ship with XP - there's no way to get rid of these accounts - hmmmm.

(2) LC4 does the "cracking" on the old LAN Manager (LM) hash technology inherited from OS/2 which is relatively trivial to break. NTLM passwords involve a relatively robust password hashing algorithm, but that advantage is removed by default because

XP automatically converts NTLM to the easily breakable LM hash for backward compatibility. Given enough time, LC4 will break every LM hash, so the "fix" is to disable the LM hash capability in the Registry and sacrifice the backward compatibility.

(3) We ran LC4 on this workstation for a bit over 16 days (57% of a complete run), and recovered all but 3 passwords. (4) Three of the passwords were cracked in less than 1 second!

(5) LC4 can be deployed over a network!!

Listed below are some common categories and a few examples of computer forensics toolkits:

1. File Viewers: Quick View Plus (http://www.jasc.com)
2. Image Viewers: ThumbsPlus http://www.cerious.com)
3. Password Crackers: l0phtcrack or LC4 (http://www.atstake.com)
4. Format-independent Text Search: dtsearch (http://www.dtsearch.com)
5. Drive Imaging: Norton Utilities' Ghost (http://www.symantec.com)
6. Complete Computer Forensics Toolkits:
    1. Forensics Toolkit (http://www.foundstone.com);
    2. ForensiX (http://www.all.net);
    3. EnCase Forensic (http://www.encase.com)
7. Forensic Computer Systems: Forensic-Computers (http://www.forensic-computers.com)
8. One of the more full-featured network tools, NetScanTools Pro (http://www.netscantools.com). Note the abundance of features built into one product!

Most computer forensics vendors offer a variety of tools, some even offer complete suites. But the links above will provide a useful, high-level overview of the world of computer forensics and the tools used therein. A cursory review of this list suggests tools that are not mainstream for the typical computer villain.

Now the rubber meets the road. We observed that the impetus for computer forensics came from law enforcement - a community that arrests, investigates, seizes, stores and locks up physical objects. The computer forensics specialist's adversary, in all likelihood, is a computer-using criminal with no particular skill level beyond that of a typical end-user. Such is not the case with Internet Forensics

A cursory review of this list of computer forensics tools suggests that they are not in widespread use by the typical computer villain. The pornographer might use a graphics tool to morph the images into something unrecognizable immediately, but that's unlikely to be anywhere near as challenging as doing a reverse-morph on an unknown file format. The computer forensics specialist works on a different plane than the person he/she is investigating.

To the contrary, the Internet Forensics specialist uses many of the same tools and engages in the same set of practices as the person he/she is investigating. Let me illustrate with a few examples.

Suppose that you've received some suspicious email, and want to verify the authenticity of a URL included within. A number of options are available. One might use a browser to access information from the American Registry for Internet Numbers (http://www.arin.net). Or one might use any number of OS utilities. But we'll save ourselves some time and worry, and use a general network appliance, NetScanTools Pro. We identified the registration, domain name servers, currency information, etc. for netscantools.com.

Now let's change the scenario slightly. Suppose that we had some hostile intent, and wanted to ferret out information about some company's network infrastructure. What tool might we use? You guessed it, NetScanTools Pro. The point is that the self-same tool is equally useful to the hacker conducting basic network reconnaissance and the legitimate Internet security specialist who's trying to determine whether a URL links to a legitimate company or a packet "booby trap." The point is that, both uses require essentially the same skill sets.

Don't get me wrong, I am not suggesting that NetScanTools Pro is a hacker tool. It is a general-purpose network analyzer. I use it all the time to analyze my networks and to explain network analysis issues to my students. But in order to serve in that capacity, it must also have the capabilities to be misused by hackers. In Internet Forensics it is customarily the case that the forensic specialist undergoes the same level of education and training as the hacker he or she seeks to thwart. The difference is one of ethics, not skill. We observed that this was not true of the perpetrator and investigator in computer forensics.

To drive home the point, look at the other options that NetScanTools Pro provides. One can use an ICMP "ping" to identify whether a particular network host is online just as easily as one can use it to identify activity periods in network reconnaissance or a network topology. One can use a Traceroute to determine network bottlenecks, or to identify intervening routers and gateways for possible man-in-the-middle attacks. One can use Port Probe to verify that a firewall is appropriately configured, or to make a list of vulnerable services on a host that may be exploited.

Where computer forensics deals with physical things, Internet forensics deals with the ephemeral. The computer forensics specialist at least has something to seize and investigate. The Internet forensics specialist only has something to investigate if the packet filters, firewalls and intrusion detection systems were set up to anticipate the breach of security. But, if one could always anticipate the breach, one could always block it. Therein lies the art, and the mystery.

If I've been successful, I've got you thinking about the fundamental differences between computer forensics and internet forensics. I think that on careful analysis, one has to conclude (a) that these are fundamentally different skills, (b) that in the case of Internet forensics, the skill sets of the successful perpetrator and successful investigator are pretty much the same, and (c) Internet forensics is as much a discipline as its search-and-seizure counterpart. This validity of these conclusions may be confirmed in any number of ways. For the most part the tools-of-the-trade for both hacker and Internet forensics specialist are the same, though the occasional extreme case like Dug Song's Dsniff http://monkey.org/~dugsong/dsniff challenges this generalization. It's hard for me to imagine a legitimate, lawful use of Dsniff's "macof" utility that enables the users to flood switch state tables! But in the main, the hacker and the Internet Forensics specialist could co-exist with the same tools and equipment.

There is also a parallel in the flow of the network traffic. Ingress traffic to the analyst is egress traffic to the hacker, v.v. The same packet crafting technique that verifies true stateful inspection of fragmented packets also launches exploits like Teardrop and Ping of Death. Indispensable tools for packet capture and analysis like tcpdump are, by definition, capable of promiscuous packet sniffing, as are intrusion detection systems like Snort. The underground hacker community and the Internet folks with the white hats are birds-of-a-feature if one ignores the direction of their moral compass. This is the time to change our focus from the negative (hacker) to the positive (Internet Forensics Specialist) dimension of this exciting new discipline, and to begin to take the differences between computer forensics and internet forensics seriously. To make the distinction complete, we need to add a few publications in Internet Forensics as SANS has already achieved near perfection in the conference arena, and GIAC already has established certification standards that seem to be universally accepted.

If we can break from the tradition of including Internet Forensics (under some name or other) as the penultimate chapter of a Computer Forensics textbook, and mislabeling the excellent word already done in the field under the theme of "reverse-hacking" we'll be well on our way to completely articulate Denning's durability, body of principles, body of practices and standards for competence, ethics and practice tests for a genuine profession.

Statistics on Internet Fraud

The Internet Crime Complaint Center http://www.spamlaws.com/reporting-internetfraud.html (IC3), a joint venture of the FBI and the National White Collar Crime Center found:

- Online auction fraud was the most reported type of fraud and accounted for 44.9% of consumers' complaints
- Non-delivered merchandise and/or payment made up 19.0% of complaints
- Check fraud represented 4.9% of complaints
- About 70% of the fraud victims were scammed through www (e.g. online auctions)
- About 30% of the victims were scammed by emails

Payment Methods

Top methods of payment used by victims of Internet fraud include:

- **Wire**

- Credit Card
- Bank Debit
- Money Order
- Check

The average loss for all Internet frauds was $1,500. More than half of these losses occurred through auctions. So protect yourself from becoming the next victim of an auction fraud. Read the tips on how to prevent auction frauds from happening to you.

Tips on How to Prevent Auction Frauds
- Learn as much as you can from the seller
- Read and examine the feedback on the seller
- Check the location of the seller. If the seller is abroad and a problem arises it will be harder to solve.
- Ask if shipping and delivery are included in the price so you receive no unexpected or additional costs.
- Refuse to give the seller your social security number or driver's license number to prevent identity theft. In fact get used to saying "no" to information requests on the Internet.

Chapter 3 - Useful tools for the "Amateur Internet Investigating Sleuth"

Useful tools for the "Amateur Internet Investigating Sleuth"
I going to give you some "amateur" tools to help you become an "amateur Internet investigator" that will assist you in finding the bad guys when they attempt or succeed in finding you.

Forensic Tools:

File Viewers:
http://www.corel.com/corel/product/index.jsp;jsessionid=SR5YpemMHxQrxjAX2FUtRA**.prd-atg-commerce8?&mapcounter=1&pid=prod4900067

Image Viewers:
http://www.cerious.com

Password Crackers:
http://www.symantec.com/specprog/atstake/index.html

Format-independent Text Search: dtsearch:
http://www.dtsearch.com

Drive Imaging: Norton Utilities' Ghost:
http://www.symantec.com

Forensics Toolkit:
http://www.foundstone.com

ForensiX:
http://www.all.net

EnCase Forensic:
http://www.guidancesoftware.com/

Forensic Computer Systems:
http://www.forensic-computers.com

NetScanTools Pro:

http://www.netscantools.com

Who owns a phone number?
http://www.freephonetracer.com/FCPT.aspx?_act=RunASearch&sou=2&cam=3282&gclid=CKPgnJTrkbkCFSJqMgod7hcAhw

Address and phone of a person
PeopleFinders:
http://www.peoplefinders.com .
Their "people search subscription" works reasonably well, finding all sorts of things, including some things that are completely wrong. Don't use this for 800 number reverse searches...I never got anything even remotely useful from those (and they will reverse the charge on these automatically if you make a mistake). For cell phone numbers doing a reverse search, it will tell you only the name of the subscriber; and the location of the number when it was originally assigned; no address of the person. It is annoying that on every search it prompts you to sign up for a $16.95 "savings" program. The link to sign up is huge. The link to say "no thanks" is below it in small type, and somewhat hard to find. I did a criminal search on a guy I knew was convicted and it wouldn't tell me what county it was in, but it did find it. This service is a bit pricey, but may be your lowest cost option if you've exhausted the alternatives.

How to find out the merchant ID of the company
You may have to put a small $ transaction through in order to get complete info. Having a rejected

transaction may only give you the "name" of the vendor as it would appear on your statement which can be quite obscure and often bogus.

Bank of America ShopSafe:
https://www.bankofamerica.com/banking-information/faq/credit-cards/faq.go
You can generate a onetime number (including the 3 digit code) that is tied to your credit card and you can set a dollar and time limit on that unique card number. But once a merchant charges to that card, it is locked to that merchant. So it is really safe.

A Visa Buxx:
http://usa.visa.com/personal/cards/prepaid/visa_buxx.html
Keep the amount in the account really low. When they try to charge your card, you can find out their merchant ID but ONLY if the transaction goes through! If it doesn't go through, then you only get the info that would appear on your bill (which could be bogus and it is not traceable). There are monthly fees though even if you don't use these cards. The B of A ShopSafe has no additional fees.

Tracking down violators

http://www.tcpalaw.com/free/track.htm
This page at tcpalaw.com is an excellent resource of all sorts of information including forms to get PO Box information.

Recording phone conversations

I use Personal call Recorder from www.digital-loggers.com. I use the free WavePad from www.nch.com.au and sample at 16000 and save it in MP3 Constant bit rate CBR 16kbps (high quality). For lower quality and fast saves, capture at 8K and save in .wav format, PCM, 8kHz, 8 bit, mon, 7Kb/sec. Be sure it is legal first:

900 numbers Number Administration System
http://www.nanpa.com/
http://www.fcc.gov/guides/900-pay-call-and-other-information-services
Report shows the responsible organization for each number. You then send a subpoena to the company to find out who owns it.

800 number ownership
As far as finding the resp org, in theory your long distance carrier should be willing to supply that for you. Ameritech has an automated service at 800-337-4194; they typically give a service number associated with the RespOrg, which you can then call to find out who the RespOrg actually is. A third method: "If you don't know who to subpoena, use the RespOrg services or go to:
http://www.fonefinder.net

Note: this works for non-toll free numbers too!) and find out the provider and then go to:
http://www.nanpa.com/number_resource_info/carrier_id_codes.html

(Download the "Feature Group D CIC assignments" zipfile) to get their contact info. Call to ask who to send a subpoena to, and then send it.

If you have a login, you can go right to the source:
http://www.sms800.com

For Canadian numbers: see CO Code Availability:
http://www.cnac.ca/mapcodes.htm
With respect to subpoenas to RespOrg, I've found that you can generally fax the subpoena to them and simply ask that they fax the answer back. In three of three cases, they have simply faxed the information back to me.

Phone number ownership
Abika services: Find out who owns a number or who is calling you:
http://www.abika.com/Reports/FindPhoneNumbers.htm
Abika offers a very comprehensive set of searches and is very similar to Docusearch. Unlike Docusearch they can trace the source of a fax call into your phone number. This is the only service we know of that lets you do that without your having to change your incoming fax line into an 800 number (they can't block their callerID if you have an incoming 800 number).

The way their service works is that you forward your fax line to their number and they forward the call back to your number instantly. In the process, they pick off the callerID that you can't get. So let's say you get 10 faxes a day. You just note the time you receive each fax and correlate it to the list they give you of phone numbers that called you at the same time. So you can identify the number of every single fax you got over any time period! It's called the "Trace Phone Calls" Search.

The Abika "Trace Phone Calls" service is highly recommended because you get the phone numbers of each of the junk faxers that called you regardless of how they are trying to block their number. Then you can use the other Abika searches to find out who they really are (billing name and address, etc). Then you can sue the sender of the faxes. This is particularly useful for pump and dump faxes and the 900 number "we want your opinion" faxes because these faxes generally never identify who is sending them (since they want to avoid lawsuits) and if they have an opt-out number, it is generally http://www.blocklist.com and that's totally useless since blocklist doesn't identify individual clients...they just give the list to all their clients. So you can't sue blocklist and blocklist can't tell you who sent the fax. In fact, someone can just list the blocklist numbers and not even be a blocklist client! So that's why the Abika service is so important and it's the only one we know of that does this.

The cost is $79.96 ($69.98 plus 9.98 processing charge) for the first month; $10 for 1 month extensions. You get 100 minutes of talk time free with your initial order. You can buy additional 60 minutes of talk time for $10 each. For Canada,

Hawaii, Alaska and Puerto Rico you get 50 minutes of talk time free with your order. You can buy additional 30 minutes of talk time for $10 each.

Note: You will probably not be able to forward back to the original number. This will depend on the local phone or Cell Phone Company and often on the area, even within the same phone company. They have a database of the phone/cell companies and the areas where it works and it does not. For areas where it gives a busy signal the call has to be returned to a different phone number or voicemail.

But for fax lines, if you don't have a second line handy or a fax machine that timestamps when the fax was really received (I don't have either), the best option is to do what I did and just forward my fax number to Abika's call center and then have them forward it the phone number of an efax service you sign up for such as http://www.efax.com. So you don't have to have another phone line installed, and you get an electronic record of everything, including accurate receipt times that you can then correlate to their call logs. And you can set everything up instantly (the efax number is instant; call forwarding may take a couple of business days to add).

Abika can immediately tell you of the caller's origin number and billing address. You either call or email them for the info. This is part of the "Trace Phone Call" monthly service. So to do a live trace, you must do the same as described above, i.e., forward your number to them and have it forwarded back.

As long as the call is 5 seconds or longer, you'll know who called you.

The service works virtually 100% of the time, even if the number is "out of area" or blocked and even when they were unidentifiable by callerID, *69, and *57. Basically, they get the ANI (Automatic Number Identification) information that certain businesses get. Getting ANI delivered real-time to your home or office requires installation of digital equipment and a separate digital line, and programming at the CO. So Abika is the quick and easy way to accomplish the same result (getting the ANI information), but without the hassle, cost, or time delay.

Here's what they write:
We have had hundreds of customers who have used our call trace. If you would like to test us out, I can activate trace for a number you specify and you can ask any of your associates to dial that number from any unlisted, anonymous phone number or even using *69 and check us out. We will trace the origin number for all calls that originate in US and Canada. The proof is in the pudding. The test will speak for itself. (Can we get the $20 for winning the bet?)

Regarding our price list, we do not have fixed pricing of our products. Our prices are dynamic and vary according to the complexity of the various searches we offer. Where is the price list? Each search is unique and gets the attention it requires. Prices vary depending on whose and what information you are searching as some information is easier (cheaper) to search and some more difficult (expensive). Once you fill out the search form with the search criteria and click "next" you will see the prices for that particular search. If the information is easy to search then that particular search is listed as FREE! You can try any of our searches. All of them have a money back guarantee for inaccurate information found. As a businessperson you would be interested in knowing that the Wall Street Journal got the full report on Richard Scrushy (ex CEO) of Healthsouth's suspect activities from us even before anyone else in the media or investment community suspected anything. The time when WSJ got the full report Healthsouth was a high flying stock. In most of the searches we offer, we have the best sources for the information. We have even had a senior editor of People Magazine, a few magazine reporters and news anchors of a couple of local TV stations use us to get information for some of their stories and personal needs.

Here are some testimonials from customers who agreed to publish their feedback:
http://www.abika.com/help/feedback.htm

You may be interested to know that we offer a similar service to trace emails and instant messages. Emails and IM traces are available for the whole of N. America, W. Europe, India, South Africa and the Pacific Rim Countries including Australia and Japan. I wonder when many of the so

called tech gurus say that emails and IM's are untraceable. We have conducted thousands of these traces with a success rate of more than 98%. A few major corporations use us to trace emails and IM's.
If you have any more questions or need any more information please do not hesitate to contact us online help@abika.com. Or if you choose you can call us at: 720-207-0362.

Docusearch:
http://www.docusearch.com/
Use Docusearch to lookup License plate owners, social security numbers lookup (for creditors) and find out who owns an 800 number, regular phone number, and more. Expensive (well under $100), but some stuff you can only get this way. If they can't find it, there's no charge. Also use Ameritech's automated RespOrg ID service: 800-337-4194.

Call trap procedure
This is guaranteed to get your offender. Have the phone company put a "trap" on the line, make note of when the calls came in. You must have the EXACT time of each call. Then I report it by calling the Annoyance and Tracking line. For SBC, the number is 800-698-7223. After you get two faxes from the same sender, if they can't get a number, then they can put traps at the remote location and eventually you get them. Hit 0 to speak a live person when calling the SBC number.

Here is some more info on call trap: Caller ID and My Privacy:
https://www.privacyrights.org/fs/fs19-cid.htm

The number for the SBC Annoyance call bureau is 925-867-8101, for example. Here's some slightly conflicting advice: Now *all* calls are logged by the LEC's (Local Exchange Carrier) computers. Ask them (via subpoena) for a call detail report (CDR) for all calls into and out from your number on the affected date. *ALL* the phone companies have this data... most for 90 days of history or more. If they tell you they don't, they are lying

Accurint.com:
http://www.accurint.com/

25-cents a search. Highly useful for tracking down people, even with unlisted phone numbers. Accurint uses a name, past address, phone number or Social Security Number to obtain the current name, address and phone number of targeted subjects. Be careful that you don't lookup someone you don't have a legal reason to lookup, or you can be sued by that person. So if you are looking up information for a lawsuit, that's ok.

Whois Source - Wildcard Domain Search Lookup
http://www.whois.sc/
I have a silver membership here. It's totally worth it if you look up website registration. There are other lots of other reverse lookup tools here if you are a member.

Advanced Research, Inc. - Background Investigations, Asset Searches, Telephone Records, Locates:
http://www.advsearch.com/
They will find a bank account owned by the debtor, bank balances for all accounts in a given bank, bank transactions, credit card transactions, Canadian phone records, etc. Even international bank account searches. You can find out where the person is currently employed. Searches that is not available on the traditional databases.

MelissaData address lookups:
http://www.melissadata.com/Lookups/index.htm

Free People Search - Find People - Free People Locator
http://www.skipease.com/

Find anyone! We'll locate missing persons, debtors, assets, and employment:
http://www.skiptracepros.com/

Satellite photos - You can search by latitude/longitude, street address, zip code, or well known locations:
http://mapper.acme.com/

International business name search

General Guides:

Company Registrars - Register of Companies - Trade, Industry
http://www.scottishlaw.org.uk/corporate/registrars.html

International Company name search
http://www.damonlegal.com/link_to_forms.htm

International phone number search
International phonebooks directory
http://www.phonebooks.com/international-phone-book.html

International Telephone Numbers Directory - City, State, Country Phone Number Look-up
http://www.searchdetective.net/

Batch reverse phone number
Use Accurint batch mode or a service from infoUSA.com.
http://list.infousa.com/cgi-bin/abicgi/abicgi.pl?bas_session={bas_session}&bas_elements=4&bas_vendor=190000&bas_type=LC&bas_page=6999&bas_action=dataproc

ABA number lookup
ABA routing number verification; free bank routing number search tool:
http://yourfavorite.com/checkwriter/verify.htm

Bank account balance: See if funds are in the account you want to levy!
http://bettercheck.com/

TCPALaw investigation tools
A great list: Tracking down violators
http://www.tcpalaw.com/free/track.htm

Report bogus domain information
Bogus information in the domain registration in violation of ICANN regulations. Registrars are required to ensure that registration data is complete & accurate. You will have to subpoena the registrar for the information on who paid for the registration. You should also download and capture all information off of the web site and look to see who hosts the web page, as they can also be subpoenaed for customer data. In the meantime, you can report incomplete or inaccurate domain registration information here:
http://wdprs.internic.net/

CorpAmerica Corporate filings

http://www.corpamerica.com/cam/Error.html?pageNotFound=%2Fcam%2Fproducts_%26_services%2F
If you want to find out who the officers are, etc. you can order a "plain" copy of corporate records for any state in the US and some foreign corporations. See also:

Division of Corporations - Authorized Direct Web Vendors:
http://www.corp.delaware.gov/directwebvend.shtml

Yellow pages, white pages, and reverse number lookup:

http://www.anywho.com/
http://www.argali.com/
Forward and reverse phone number lookup. This is a downloadable FREE tool that searches public databases.

FCC unsolicited fax orders and search:
http://transition.fcc.gov/eb/tcd/ufax.html
Enter the name your favorite spammer and read what the FCC has done about them. Our favorite spammer, fax.com has 6 separate FCC citations on this page alone! This site uses the search engine that I invented when I was CEO of Infoseek, by the way. The FCC citations explain the law much better than anything I've seen on other sites. Read a few of them to educate yourself on the law.

GEEKTOOLS Whois Proxy
http://www.geektools.com/whois.php
Fast whois lookup

Cell Phone Magic:
http://www.cell-phone-numbers.com/
They will find out who owns a cell phone.
This online store offers a variety of searches and stuff you won't find anywhere else....like how to get keys for the car you want to levy.
http://www.ioffer.com/

US SEARCH:
http://www.ussearch.com/consumer/index.jsp
Similar to Docusearch

Offering nationwide and international investigative services, spy gadgets, safety and surveillance products, records research, criminal background checks and personal information verification services. Information retrieval for insurance companies, law firms, repossession agents, financial institutions, collection agencies, private investigators, bounty hunters, process servers, bail bondsmen, businesses, spouses and parents.

Excellent maildrop search: Mail boxes - remailing services. Directory of mail drops and mail boxes:
http://www.maildropguide.com/go/

Who is at this Address?
If I have an address and I am not sure what it is, or if it's even a real address, then I always go to http://www.usps.com and look up the address and the post office that delivers to the address. Then I call that post office and ask them if they know what's located at that address. I ask if it is a residential address, or if it's an office building of some sort. I ask them if they know if the address is a Commercial Mail Receiving Agency (CMRA) like a Mailboxes Etc or UPS Store. The post office is not required to answer these types of questions, but they can if they want to. I'd say 90% of the time they tell me what I need to know.

FEIN number lookup
Federal Employer ID Number can found here if it is registered:
http://www.Knowx.com

FEIN Number information Search Corporation Tax ID Number
https://www.knowx.com/fein/search.jsp
http://www.dnb.com

AutoTrackXP:
https://clear.thomsonreuters.com/
Very comprehensive searches! Requires a subscription agreement and qualification.

Reverse Phone Directory - Find Name and Street Address from Telephone Number
http://www.reversephonedirectory.com/

Reverse phone number lookup:
http://www.infospace.com/ispace/ws/index

Find out who owns a phone number
Reverse Address Directory - Lookup Street Address Find Person's Name and

Telephone Number to Locate People and See Who Lives There.
http://www.reverseaddress.com/

Craig Ball's Sampler of Informal Discovery Links:
http://www.craigball.com/
A pretty extensive list of resources

ScreenNow:
https://employment.fadv.com/pub/
Get all sorts of info on a person.

Net Detective 2001 people search utility software- HDP Corporate Website
http://ndet.jeanharris.com/
Essentially a bunch of semi-useful hyperlinks, all categorized for you

OnlineDetective.com - unlisted phone numbers dmv records detectives personal public records investigate anything and more!
http://www.onlinedetective.com/
Seems to be similar to net detective

SuperPages.com:
http://www.superpages.com/
A search at superpages.com (hint: I usually look for the category "mail" at the particular address, then if that doesn't turn up a mail drop, search for any businesses at the address) turns up, for example, 5401 Chimney Rock Apartments 5401 Chimney Rock Road, Houston, TX 77081 (713) 661-3790

Canada phone number lookup
http://www.canada411.ca/
Canada's 411

United States Postal Service - ZIP + 4 Lookup
https://www.usps.com/
Handy when they don't give you enough info to confirm you got the right company.

GNU wget:
http://www.gnu.org/software/wget/wget.html

I used this to grab a complete copy of the fax.com website so that they couldn't change it.

Find out who owns a PO Box:
http://www.junkfax.org/fax/misc/pobox.htm
Some popular techniques to find out the owner of PO Box

Telephone Prefix location:
http://www.thedirectory.org/pref/
If you have a phone number like (650) 423-xxxx, it will tell you where that phone is.

CCS International Ltd: Surveillance, Counter surveillance and Hi-Tech Spy and

Security Products:
http://www.spyzone.com/

GSM, CELLULAR, COMPUTER, FAX MONITORING
http://www.gcomtech.com/
Due to federal law, you must be in law enforcement to get access to this site.

ZoomInfo:
http://www.zoominfo.com/
This is a free site where you can find lots of information about a person or a company gathered from analyzing web pages. Very impressive!

Find out who called you

Use the call trace feature offered by the phone company. I did a *57 and got a "successful" trace, FWIW, plus an announcement that for $8 (plus tax and tip, no doubt) I can even have it reported to the police. For $8, they can record the number. Then if you take action, you subpoena the phone company for the call info, and if it is a subscriber of that phone company, you get info on the caller as well. If it's not a subscriber of the phone co, you generally get who the local carrier is so you know who to subpoena for the subscriber info. If you were to have the number but want the subscriber info, and issued a subpoena to SWB, they would charge you a $25 fee for the record search. When you do a call trace, you get the whole shebang for $8. I've done call traces when I have the subscriber's name and number, but want a) a sworn affidavit from the phone company saying that the call was made from number "X" to my number "Y" at a specific date and time, and b) if it is from a SWB customer, full ID of the calling party, including name & address where the service is installed. All for $8, much cheaper than issuing a subpoena for records after the fact, and with more info.

Locating a company
http://www.residentagentinfo.com
http://www.checkemout.com/corporation_go.html
has a nationwide corp/dba search for $39.00.
http://www.freelancesecurity.com will let you have private PI's bid for a service you describe.

Can We Tape?

http://www.rcfp.org/taping/
Rules regarding taping of phone conversations in each state.

Subpoena information
The AT&T Subpoena Center 800-291-4952 (voice) 248-552-1764 (fax)
Southwestern Bell, SBC is now AT&T Teleport Communications Group (TCG) is now AT&T Corporate Security (Subpoena Compliance) 800-732-5689 800-559-7928 (general information) Must mail subpoena to: AT&T c/o CT Corporation Systems 1515 Market Street, Suite 1210 Philadelphia, PA 19102

I was told that they charge $150 for subscriber information, but that they will refund that money if they simply rebill service to another telephone service provider. One time they looked up a number that I gave them on the phone and told me it was rebilled to ICG Telecom Group, so I didn't need to send a subpoena at all.

Southwestern Bell, SBC is now AT&T Pac/Pacific Bell is http:www.sbc.com, 800-750-2355 Subpoena Department is 800-291-4952 (1, 5) 208 S. Akard, 10th Floor Dallas, TX 75202 214-464-2854 (fax) They said that they won't respond to a civil subpoena from out of state unless I have a search warrant or make a request on a federal level.

AT&T long distance and RespOrg information 877-973-7767, 2 Send subpoena's for toll free numbers to VP Regulatory Long Distance 5850 West Los Positas Boulevard, Room 302 Pleasanton, CA 94588 I sent a subpoena to AT&T the West Los Positas address and it was responded to by SBC Southwest at the South Akard address. I also sent one that never got a response.

Chapter 4 - Online Resources

Center for Democracy and Technology. Impact of the McCain-Kerrey Bill on Constitutional Privacy Rights.
http://www.cdt.org/crypto/legis_105/mccain_kerrey/const_impact.html

CERIAS: Digital Forensics Resources.
http://www.cerias.purdue.edu/research/forensics/resources.php?output=printable

Computer Crime and Intellectual Property Section Criminal Division, United States Department of Justice. Searching and Seizing Computers and Obtaining Electronic Evidence in Criminal Investigations.

http://www.justice.gov/criminal/cybercrime/

Computer Forensics, Cybercrime and Steganography Resources
http://www.forensics.nl/links/

Computer Forensics World.
http://www.computerforensicsworld.com

Computer Professionals for Social Diversity: Computer Crime Directory.
http://www.cpsr.org/

Cornell University. Federal Rules of Evidence.
http://www.law.cornell.edu/rules/fre/overview.html

Craiger, J. Philip. Computer Forensics Procedures and Methods.
http://www.ncfs.ucf.edu/craiger.forensics.methods.procedures.final.pdf

Forensics Information from CERT
http://www.cert.org/forensics/

The Forensics Science Portal
http://www.forensics.ca/index.php

Ghosh, Ajoy. Guidelines for the Management of IT Evidence.
http://unpan1.un.org/intradoc/groups/public/documents/APCITY/UNPAN016411.pdf

Kessler International - Forensic Accounting, Computer Forensics, Corporate Investigation.
http://www.investigation.com/praccap/hightech/compforen.htm

National Center for Forensic Science.
http://www.ncfs.ucf.edu/digital_evd.html

Nolan, Richard, et. al. Forensics Guide to Incident Response for Technical Staff.
http://www.cert.org/archive/pdf/FRGCF_v1.3.pdf

Robbins, Judd. An Explanation of Computer Forensics.
http://www.computerforensics.net/

Sergienko, Greg S. Self Incrimination and Cryptographic Keys.
http://law.richmond.edu/jolt/v2i1/sergienko.html#h1

Printed Resources

Casey, Eoghan. Digital Evidence and Computer Crime (Second Edition). San Diego, CA:
Academic Press, 2000.
Farmer, Dan; Venema, Wietse. Forensic Discovery. Addison-Wesley Professional, 2005.
Nelson, Bill. Guide to Computer Forensics and Investigations. Boston, MA: Thomson
Course Technology, 2004.

Forensic Resources

FINDING PEOPLE FOR FREE:
Directory Services:
Craig's Phone Finder
http://www.craigball.com/phonefind.html
Performs parallel search of other directory services, including Yahoo, WhoWhere, Switchboard, Infospace, AnyWho and Worldpages, plus reverse searches by phone # or address and map links.

MelissaData Lookup Directory
http://www.melissadata.com/Lookups/index.htm
This eclectic melange of lookups isn't going to make you Sherlock (or Shirley) Holmes, but it's a useful compendium of free data. Thanks to Lee Keller King for the suggestion

AnyWho
http://www.anywho.com/
A simple, fast way to search over 100 million directory listings. More up-to-date than some.

Bankruptcy Locator
http://www.pacer.gov/
This free search will tell you whether the individual or business name you enter is listed in a bankruptcy filing since January 1992. This search will tell you the date, name, city and state.

Bigfoot
http://www.bigfoot.com/
So-so white pages, yellow pages, web pages and e-mail searches.

Information USA
http://www.infousa.com/
Listings for 113 million households and 10 million businesses

Info Space
http://www.infospace.com/
Search telephone directories in USA, Canada and other countries. Also yellow pages search, E-mail finder, corporate directory, Toll free number database, fax number database, and government telephone number directory. An excellent, wide-ranging site.

Switchboard
http://www.switchboard.com/
A simple, quick way to find almost anyone, anywhere who has a listed phone number.

WhoWhere
http://www.whowhere.com/
Find E-mail addresses and phone numbers from among 90 million U.S. listings. Also, toll-free numbers, yellow pages and corporate web site locator

WorldPages
http://www.beta.yellowbook.com/?beta=betaV10
Links to 112 million U.S. and Canadian white and yellow pages listings, but most valuable for its links to over 200 directories worldwide.

YAHOO People Search

http://www.yahoo.com/search/people/email.html
Conduct surname searches via a national cris-cross directory. Locate E-mail addresses, home pages and phone numbers.

Reverse Directory Services:
Reverse Directory: InfoUSA
http://www.infousa.com/
Both a people finder and a reverse directory: If you know the phone number, this database will return the subscriber's name and address

Reverse Directory: InfoSpace
http://www.infospace.com/
This directory offers reverse lookup by phone number, fax number, U.S. street address and e-mail address!

Resources for Finding People:

Birthday Database
http://anybirthday.com/
Over 130 million birthdays online in a free searchable database. Search by name, limit by zip code.

Social Security Death Index
http://search.ancestry.com/search/db.aspx?dbid=3693
Find information about persons whose death triggered a Social Security benefit (e.g., social security number, dates of birth and death and place of residence).

Black Book Online
http://www.crimetime.com/online.htm
A helpful, free collection of links to investigative resources warns that it is "for professional investigators ONLY. If you are not a private investigator, or in the legal, insurance, collection, journalistic or law enforcement professions."

Search Systems Public Record Locator
http://www.searchsystems.net/
This comprehensive links list is free, well-organized and includes many gems. It's definitely worth a look.

"Searching for People" page
http://www.searchingforpeople.com/

Links to resources for finding people
Missing Persons Resource Center
http://www.pimall.com/nais/missingm.html

Articles and book descriptions on professional methods for skip tracing.
Webgator
http://www.virtualgumshoe.com/
Excellent list of online investigative resources

FEE BASED INVESTIGATIVE RESOURCES

Accurint
http://www.accurint.com/

The newest kid on the block for skip tracing. What sets it apart is not just the high quality of its data, but its pricing: just dirt cheap. Accurint can find people for a quarter and will deliver a neat little dossier of addresses, relatives, neighbors and more in seconds, for under five bucks. The interface is intuitive and intelligent, and the system allows users to track usage by account or client number and authorize use by others within an account. The owner of the account can set additional user IDs and passwords, as well as program access limits for authorized sub-users. Although currently geared to not much more than skip tracing, UCC filings and phone numbers, Accurint expects to be adding drivers' license records for thirty-three states along with criminal records data. On a scale from one to wow, Accurint is a WOW!

Public Data
http://www.publicdata.com/
This inexpensive but increasingly dated database contains records of licensed drivers, sex offenders, voters, vehicle license tags, criminal records and voter rolls. Search license records by name or DL # and learn name, address, weight, birth date, sex, expiration date, status, class and restrictions. Although principally a Texas resource, it also offers DMV and/or DL information for Florida, Idaho, Iowa, Maine, Mississippi, Minnesota, Ohio, Oregon, South Dakota, Utah and Wyoming.

US Search
http://www.ussearch.com/

This heavily-publicized company does a reasonably good job of skip-tracing and background checking. They are pleasant and helpful, while offering a very quick turnaround and live telephone support outside regular business hours.

Information for Business
http://www.info4business.com/
A reliable resource with reasonable prices and toll-free telephone support. This well-run outfit offers just about any type of data you could want and an impressive turnaround time for basic reports. The helpful people give this service an edge. Highly recommended.

Intelius
http://www.intelius.com/
This attractive and well-organized site offers the full range of skip-trace and asset identification data. Be warned that some of the data they are offering for sale is currently available online without charge (e.g., Social Security death records, surname searches, OSHA reports, FAA records, etc.).

Texas Department of Public Safety Convictions Records Database
http://records.txdps.state.tx.us/
This site allows you to obtain information about criminal conviction and felony deferred adjudication records maintained by the Texas Department of Public Safety. Courts and criminal justice agencies throughout the state submit these records to DPS.

Searches cost $3.15 each and you can pay online with a credit card.

InformUs
http://www.informus.com/
Driving records nationwide, Workers' comp. claim searches in 40 States, criminal records nationwide, previous employment verifications in 72 hours, national credit and address information.
FREE to check validity and state/time of issuance for any S.S. #.

KnowX
http://www.knowx.com/
A reasonably priced (and partially free) search engine for millions of public records, including real property ownership, bankruptcies, assets, UCC filings and many more.

Locate Fast
http://www.loc8fast.com/
Claims to have a billion records online. $1.75 per credit header search (name, SS#, address, phone).

LocateMe
http://locateme.com/
Search selected public records (principally voter and DMV records) of all 50 states for $39.00 per search.

National Association of Investigative Specialists
http://www.pimall.com/nais/home.html

A fascinating conglomeration of investigative resources, spy equipment, skip trace resources, P.I. publications, etc.

SEARCH ENGINES

Craig Ball's Search Central
http://www.craigball.com/searchcentral.html
Use all major search engines via one simple interface. Not selling anything!

Google
http://www.google.com/
This is the best search engine in the world. A very fast, often relevant search engine that is less likely than some to be misled by metatags and other techniques used to draw users to sites.

Dogpile
http://www.dogpile.com/
This inelegantly-named site permits simultaneous searches of every part of the Internet using all major search engines

Yahoo
http://www.yahoo.com/
Topical search engine. Very user friendly.

Beaucoup
http://www.beaucoup.com/
Extraordinarily comprehensive links to all manner of search engines (over 800 listed) and reference

sources. Perhaps the ultimate in one-stop searching.

Savvy Search
http://www.savvysearching.com/
Another parallel search engine that allows you to check 17 major search resources in one fell swoop.

SEARCH NEWSGROUPS AND MAILING LISTS

Google Groups
http://groups.google.com/
Search through Email in USENET newsgroups and mailing lists for specific subjects. You can sift through more than 40,000 discussion forums, plus newsgroups and mailing lists (700,000,000 messages!).

CHECK OUT CORPORATIONS AND ASSOCIATIONS

Tax Exempt Organizations
http://www.irs.gov/Charities-&-Non-Profits/Search-for-Charities
Search the IRS' directory of tax exempt organizations by name, city and state.

Hoover's Corporate Information
http://www.hoovers.com/
Profiles of corporations (some free, some fee-based) and relevant links. An excellent first stop for corporate information.

Lexis

http://www.lexis.com/
The old familiar legal research tool is a superb way to identify the registered agent for service of process and other key information about any registered corporation, PA or PC. Goto TXSOS (for Texas Secretary of State Records) (Fee based). You can search Lexis and Nexis via the Internet if you are a current subscriber by using the URL: telnet://nex.lexis-nexis.com/ Tell them your terminal type is ".vt100"

SEC EDGAR Archives
http://www.sec.gov/cgi-bin/srch-edgar
Online corporate filings with the U.S. Securities and Exchange Commission.

CHECK OUT INSURANCE COMPANIES

A. M. Best
http://www.ambest.com/
Address, phone number and rating for insurance companies

Insure.com
http://www.insure.com/index2.html
Ostensibly unbiased consumer information about auto, home and life insurance, including insurance company ratings from Standard & Poor's - Includes insurance links by state and a library of carrier lawsuits.

CHECK OUT LAWYERS

Martindale-Hubble

http://www.martindale.com/
The online version of the ubiquitous lawyer's decorative books - MH lets you find just about any lawyer in America.

West's Legal Directory
http://lawyers.findlaw.com/lawyer/lawyer_dir/search/jsp/name_search.jsp
Offers basic information on over 800,000 lawyers. Yikes!

PLANES, TRAINS, BOATS, TRUCKS & AUTOMOBILES

Aviation Databases
http://www.aviationdatabases.com/
An extensive collection of searchable databases of aircraft ownership, registration, pilot licensure, etc.

Coast Guard Vessel Database
http://www.st.nmfs.noaa.gov/st1/CoastGuard/VesselByName.html
Search the United States Coast Guard's database of vessels (crafts >5tons) by vessel name. To search by vessel I.D. number, click here.

Commercial Interstate Carriers
http://www.safersys.org/
Search the Department of Transportation's SAFER database. Searchable by firm name, DOT Number and Motor Carrier number. If you catch the D.O.T. number stenciled on the cab of a tractor trailer, you

can use this database to get the truck's owner, insurance carrier, and crashes in the last two years.

Air Transport data
http://www.bts.gov/
The Bureau of Transportation Statistics Office of Airline Information (OAI) database

Airworthiness Directives
http://av-info.faa.gov/
Contains malfunction and defect reports on aircraft and parts.

NTSB Accident Briefs
http://www.ntsb.gov/
A searchable database of National Transportation Safety Board aircraft accident briefs

NHTSA
http://www.nhtsa.gov/
National Highway Traffic Safety Administration. Regulations, standards, recalls and a host of other automotive safety information.

NHTSA Recalls
http://1.usa.gov/
Information on recalled vehicles, organized by year and model.

US Dept. of Transportation
http://www.dot.gov/
Handsome site links to government agencies with oversight function for trains, planes, automobiles

and boats. Search a massive library and regulatory database. A great resource.

Accident Reconstruction Resources
http://www.c-design.com/accrec.html
Extensive list of Internet links, addresses and phone numbers of accident reconstruction resources, including reconstruction software packages

Kelly Blue Book
http://www.kbb.com/
How much is that car worth? FREE online access to the massive market value database (both wholesale and retail values available)

PRODUCTS LIABILITY, ET AL.

ATSDR
http://www.atsdr.cdc.gov/
The Agency for Toxic Substances and Disease Registry offers Data on toxic and hazardous substances

U.S. Dept. of Labor's Occupational Safety & Health Admin.
http://www.osha.gov/
Complete OSHA standards online, plus links to other safety and health sites.

Material Safety Data Sheets
https://www.msds.com/
Alphabetical compilation of Material Safety Data Sheets for virtually any compound.

Consumer Product Safety Commission
http://www.cpsc.gov/
The US Consumer Product Safety Comm. shares recall info and publications. This site is especially good for toy safety advisories.

Construction Criteria Base
http://www.ccb.org/
An online construction industry library detailing codes, standards, specification and documentation of every stripe pertaining to the construction industry. Subscription only except for free access to the Unified Facilities Guide Specifications.

The Consumer Law Page Defective Product Resource Page
http://www.consumer-action.org/links/articles/the_consumer_law_page
This useful compilation of resources (primarily geared to promote California's The Alexander Law Firm), offers a host of information about defective products and lists many links to other resources.

Intellectual Property Resources
http://www.patents.com/
"One stop shopping" for online patent and trademark resources

Delphion Patent Server
https://www2.delphion.com/cgi-bin/ncommerce3/ExecMacro/IPN/IPNmandreg.d2w/report

Database of millions of U.S. Patent & Trademark Office patent descriptions from 1971 to present, and graphics from 1790 to present. Search for patents by number or by words in the inventor, title, abstract, assignee, agent, and claims fields. Each patent links to all others in that classification. Also contains data on foreign patents. Limited free access.

MEDICAL

Craig's Managed Care Links
http://www.craigball.com/hotlinks.html
A concise list of links of use to persons litigating managed care liability cases.

American Medical Association
http://www.ama-assn.org/
Offers online member database

PubMed
http://www.ncbi.nlm.nih.gov/PubMed/
The Nat'l Library of Medicine gives FREE access to the 12 million+ citations in MedLine.

Medscape
http://www.medscape.com/
Medscape offers free access to Medline, Toxline and Merriam-Webster's Medical Desk Dictionary, as well as tens of thousands of full-text articles covering a range of medical specialties. An excellent, fast-growing and easy-to-use resource. Think of it as "Yahoo M.D."

Merck Manual
http://www.merck.com/pubs/mmanual/
The Merck Manual of Diagnosis and Therapy, now in its 17th edition, is the best all-around medical reference source out there. Thank you Merck & Co.

New England Journal of Medicine
http://www.nejm.org/
Non-subscribers have access to abstracts of online articles back to 1975 and full text of articles more than six months old.

The Visible Human
http://www.nlm.nih.gov/research/visible/
They froze some folks solid, scanned the heck out of them, sliced them up thinner than pastrami and photographed it all. An amazing, massive database of anatomical information and stunning pictures.

BANKING
American Bankers Association
http://www.aba.com/
One of American banking's most influential lobbying organization. Banking links, products, services and professional education.

List of Bank Internet Sites
http://www.thecommunitybanker.com/bank_links/
This site claims to link to over 95% of all online bank sites.

American Banker Online

http://www.americanbanker.com/
Headlines, financial data and a free two week trial subscription.

Federal Deposit Insurance Corporation
http://www.fdic.gov/
This comprehensive site offers much of use to commercial bankers, including downloadable FFIEC forms, full-text searching of FDIC rules and regulations and detailed financial data on individual banks (making it easier to keep an eye on the competition).

National Information Center
http://www.ffiec.gov/nic/
The Fed's National Information Center of Banking Information. Offers data on bank organizational structures and finances.

Currency Exchange Rates
http://www.ratesfx.com/
Daily unofficial average cross rates for major international currencies. Slick, but easy to use.

Banking Law Online
http://www.law.cornell.edu/topics/banking.html
Why waste money on high-priced lawyers? Free online access to the text of Federal and state bank regulations and federal appellate decisions. Read it and you'll quickly realize why you hire the lawyers.

Bank Rate Monitor
http://www.bankrate.com/

Geared to consumers of banking services, offers mortgage, home equity loan, savings, credit card and checking account rates. Also tracks ATM fees and online banking fees for >2,500 institutions, surveyed weekly in 117 mkts and 50 states.

Credit Unions
http://www.ncua.gov/
The National Credit Union Administration is an independent federal agency that supervises and insures 6,814 federal credit unions and insures 4,181 state-chartered credit unions.

ACCOUNTING

SmartPros Accounting
http://www.accountingnet.com/
Billing itself as "the complete online resource for accounting professionals," this energetic site includes an online research facility and a thriving forum for accounting professionals (recent topic: "Are accountants stuffy or is it me?"),

American Institute of CPAs
http://www.aicpa.org/
Conference information, a wealth of online publication and industry news and a comprehensive links page save this otherwise dry-as-dust site.

AuditNet Resource List
http://www.auditnet.org/

An excellent overview of online accounting resources. If it's in English, on the 'Net somewhere and concerns accounting, it's probably listed here.

IRS Tax Forms and Publications
http://www.irs.gov/uac/Forms,-Publications,-and-Other-Tax-Products
If forced to say something nice about the Service, I'd mention its website. All the major reporting forms and publications are online here, in Adobe Acrobat (PDF) "file ready" format.

IRS Tax Regulations
http://www.irs.gov/Tax-Professionals/Tax-Code,-Regulations-and-Official-Guidance
Although not the easiest site to navigate, the regulations are all here.

MAPS

Expedia Maps
http://www.expediamaps.com/
Microsoft modestly calls this site "the best resource for online maps." It's not. I guess if the map is wrong, Bill Gates buys the town and moves it.

MapQuest
http://www.mapquest.com/
Free atlas, personalized maps of any location and driving directions

Map-Related Websites

http://www.lib.utexas.edu/maps/map_sites/map_sites.html
Comprehensive list of online map resources. This is a map lover's paradise!

MapBlast
http://www.mapblast.com/
Another good site that gives you a map if you give it an address, or even an intersection.

TRAVEL

Savvy Traveler
http://www.dianaball.net/
Okay, I'm biased. This is my wife's link site, but that doesn't change the fact that it's an intelligent and handy resource for the savvy traveler (or the person who wants to be one).

Concierge.com
http://www.concierge.com/
The online realm of Conde Nast Traveler magazine. A lovely photo gallery, useful online forums and editor's choices make this site special.

Expedia
http://www.expedia.com/
Microsoft's online travel planner. It offers some fine features, including flight status information and 360 degree travel views.

Fodor's Travel Online
http://www.fodors.com/

An excellent site, especially useful for locating restaurants and hotels and for travel tips. But, you have to wonder why Houston --the 4th largest city in the US-- is omitted entirely!

Frommer's
http://www.frommers.com/
This "Outspoken Encyclopedia of Travel" principally promotes the many books and resources in the Arthur Frommer series. Still, very useful.

Rick Steves' Europe Through the Back Door
http://www.ricksteves.com/
Public TV's goofy travel guru knows his stuff when it comes to enjoying Europe on the cheap. Pack light and check this site (especially the comments in the "graffiti" section) before you go.

Realtime Flight Tracking
http://flightaware.com/
Free, up-to-the-minute data on planes in flight between major U.S. cities. Superimposed on a weather map. Very cool!

Travelocity
http://www.travelocity.com/
Good all-round general database and a good place to start to check flight connections, prices and availability.

Yahoo Travel
http://travel.yahoo.com/

Yahoo's portal to travel information is characteristically simple and includes reservation links. Although it boasts a few travel goodies, this site remains little more than a search engine, and only tangentially a content provider.

FEDEX
http://www.fedex.com/us/tracking/
Track FedEx packages by airbill number. Query: If you get something from the opposition, can you run sequential airbill numbers to see to whom else they are sending FedEx packages? Probably a real bad idea, ethically speaking.

UPS
http://www.ups.com/
Track any UPS bar-coded shipment and find out where it is at this very moment.

E-Bay
http://www.ebay.com/
What can I say? I'm an e-Bay junkie. This online auction lists over 3.8 million items for sale. A cautious buyer can get incredible deals. If you collect anything, e-Bay will likely prove the best, cheapest source for what you seek.

Political Contributions
http://www.tray.com/FECInfo/index.html-ssi
Search Federal Election Commission records of political contributions. Which way do you suppose the judge leans if she gave $1,000.00 to "The Newt?"

Automatic Translator
http://extensions.joomla.org/extensions/languages/automatic-translations
You've got to love this! Enter any text, or even the URL of a web page, and this free service automatically translates it to or from Spanish, French, German, Italian or Portuguese.

Webcams
http://www.steveweb.com/
One of many Webcam link pages. "Around the World in Eighty Clicks" links to real-time images of people and places all over the world.

FACSNET
http://www.facsnet.org/
Master directory of online resources used by news reporters (most are fee-based services)

OTHER LINKS PAGES

Search Systems
http://www.searchsystems.net/
Okay, I'm impressed. More than 8,800 free public data resources linked from this site, sensibly indexed both topically and geographically. Somebody deserves a medal for this one!

Attorney's Toolbox
http://www.macattorney.com/tools.html
An interesting and useful hodge-podge of sites assembled by a California attorney

CEOExpress
http://www.ceoexpress.com/
CEOExpress is comprehensive, quick and easy. A great resource!

WashLaw WEB
http://www.washlaw.edu /
This simple interface (by Washburn Univ. Law School) leads to a huge body of legal research resources.

Chapter 5 - I Have a Special Gift for My Readers

I appreciate my readers for without them I am just another struggling author attempting to make ends meet.

My readers and I have in common a passion for the written word as well as the desire to learn and grow from books.

My special offer to you is a massive ebook library that I have compiled over the years. It contains hundreds of fiction and non-fiction ebooks in Adobe Acrobat PDF format as well as the Greek classics and old literary classics too.

In fact, this library is so massive to completely download the entire library will require over 5 GBs open on your desktop.

Use the link below and scan all of the ebooks in the library. You can select the ebooks you want individually or download the entire library.

The link below does not expire after a given time period so you are free to return for more books rather than clog your desktop. And feel free to give the link to your friends who enjoy reading too.

I thank you for reading my book and hope if you are pleased that you will leave me an honest review so that I can improve my work and or write books that appeal to your interests.

Okay, here is the link…

http://tinyurl.com/special-readers-promo

PS: If you wish to reach me personally for any reason you may simply write to mailto:support@epubwealth.com.

I answer all of my emails so rest assured I will respond.

Meet the Author

Dr. Leland Benton is Director of Applied Web Info, a leading Internet Marketing company based in Utah. With over 21,000 resellers in over 22-countries, its operating entity - Neternatives.com - is a leader in Information Technology and online marketing. He is also a behavioral scientist and Chief Forensics Investigator for ForensicsNation.com. Leland resides in Southern Utah.

Visit some of his websites
http://appliedmindsciences.com/
http://appliedwebinfo.com/
http://bookbuilderplus.com
http://embarrassingproblemsfix.com/
http://www.epubwealth.com/
http://forensicsnation.com/
http://www.freebiesnation.com/
http://neternatives.com/
http://privacynations.com/
http://survivalnations.com/
http://thebentonkitchen.com
http://theolegions.org

Some Other Books You May Enjoy from ePubWealth...

FNC Bushwhacker Program $2.99
Kindle Version
http://www.amazon.com/dp/B007I9AHVS

PDF Version
https://www.paypal.com/cgi-bin/webscr?cmd=_s-xclick&hosted_button_id=KMKHDMBQSZ4E4

Have you ever been hacked? Have you been a victim of Identity Theft? Has your computer ever been infected with a virus, malware, or spyware? Do you know who is reading your personal information, spying on your cell phone conversations and text messages?

The Internet is a fantastic tool that we all have come to rely on for a vast variety of needs but the Internet is a cesspool of cyber-crime and hackers bent on evil intent. From child predators that prey on kids in chat rooms to corporate espionage where corporate secrets are pilfered and sold for sizeable profits, cyber-crime is real and the cyber-criminals are very good at what they do.

How good are you at preventing them from practicing their evil trade?

The FNC Bushwhacker Program teaches you how to become the hunter instead of the prey. It also teaches you how to block cyber-criminals from accessing your personal information, protect your children, and catch the bad guys when they attempt to make you a victim.

Everyone should become a student of the FNC Bushwhacker program. It is that important!

FNC Bushwhacker Program comes in two parts.

The second part is called the FNC Bushwhacker PLUS Program is an in depth course that makes you literally bulletproof to cyber-crime of all types. It provides all of the resources you need to become an "amateur internet sleuth" and this is a must instructional experience.

You cannot afford not to be without this information!

Dropping Off The Grid $6.87
Kindle Version
http://www.amazon.com/dp/B006JLGKLC
PDF Version
https://www.paypal.com/cgi-bin/webscr?cmd=_s-xclick&hosted_button_id=X6N67JYHPLWB6

Privacy Issues – Dropping Off The Grid is all about protecting your privacy and your loved ones from such things as identity theft, data theft, and consumer fraud. The identity thief is patient and lurks in the background waiting for you to slip up. ID theft prevention is easy and this book will give you resources on how to protect yourself and loved ones from all types of internet privacy issues. It provides valuable resources to protecting your privacy in a variety of situations such as Internet, credit, business and personal.

It is the only compendium of its kind that gives you everything you need to protect your privacy and all at your fingertips. Keep the criminal elements and stalkers at bay. Protect your identity, your finances and your privacy now. This Parenting and Family book is a one that the whole family can enjoy.

Teach your children while they are young to guard their privacy. Make it a family activity. Privacy is a right! Know your consumer rights today!

Child Watch $2.99
Kindle Version
http://www.amazon.com/dp/B0095K1P3M
PDF Version
https://www.paypal.com/cgi-bin/webscr?cmd=_s-xclick&hosted_button_id=FLJM7KUKXKG6U

School Safety & Violence – Child Watch is all about protecting children from sexual predators and the many dangers they face daily. It provides true insight into cyber crimes and child predators. It was written by Chief Forensics Investigator and behavioral scientist, Dr. Leland Benton. He has spent the better part of 31-years tracking down and apprehending some of the worst child predators. No one is more qualified to tell this amazing story. If you have children then you need to read this book. If you have a desire to learn how to better protect your family and loved ones, Child Watch offers insight into the safeguards necessary to identify and block cyber criminals including sexual predators. It also identifies bullying in schools and offers bullying in schools resources and ways to stop bullying. It provides domestic violence education and ways to protect children from people they know that may harm them. Youth violence is at an all time high and Dr. Benton offers ways to prevent youth violence. He demonstrates school intervention programs and security for schools. Educate yourself in what exactly your children are facing and take steps to protect them now.

Confessions of a Child Predator $6.87
Kindle Version
http://www.amazon.com/dp/B007BB97KU
PDF Version
https://www.paypal.com/cgi-bin/webscr?cmd=_s-xclick&hosted_button_id=KJDUPJC8ZRR26

"Confessions of a Child Predator" is a hard core look inside the minds of two female child predators. As convicted sex offenders and murderers, they were serving life sentences without parole. The interview was conducted in prison by behavior scientist Dr. Harry Jay.

Parents, you need to read this book because it contains information that will amaze you. Information like how your children are exposed daily to child molesters…DAILY… and how to protect them are all in this book. It is also imperative that you use various online sex offender registry websites and conduct a sex offenders search in your local area to find registered sex offenders that live close to you. More importantly, learn the child predator warning signs and keep a constant eye on your children and their environment.

Cyber-Daters Beware $2.99
Kindle Version
http://www.amazon.com/dp/B006J9T4NA
PDF Version

https://www.paypal.com/cgi-bin/webscr?cmd=_s-xclick&hosted_button_id=M8S965D4889X8

Cyber Dating Dangers – Cyber Daters BEWARE outlines the inherent dangers of online relationships beginning at various single sites and all of the stories are taken from actual case studies. Online singles – be afraid...be real afraid! Cyber dating isn't all as safe as they want you to believe. Both men and women need to protect themselves and their online personals information. How is online dating dangerous?

Cyber-Daters BEWARE shows you the inherent dangers and how to protect yourself from the predators that lurk in the background. Online dating scams abound on these single sites. Look for the clues! This book will teach you how to identify the clues. This Advice and How To book outlines the ways to protect yourself and what to look for if you choose to cyber date. It is all about safe online dating. Parents and families should read this book together as children become of dating age.

Cyber Protect Your Business $4.87
Kindle Version
http://www.amazon.com/dp/B0095JEAYY
PDF Version
https://www.paypal.com/cgi-bin/webscr?cmd=_s-xclick&hosted_button_id=596BMEK4NM6GS

Cyber Protection – Cyber Protect Your Business is about protecting one of your most important assets

– your business and your livelihood. Statistics demonstrate that hackers are now targeting small businesses more so than individuals because the payoffs are greater and there are fewer safeguards put in place by the business owner. It is easy pickings and the business owners that take the time to read this book and implement the strategies contained herein will be the targets that the hackers ignore since there are easier targets available.

Cyber Protect Your Business is about protecting YOU and your loved ones from the silent menaces that plow the web and seek to harm you. Learn about internet surveillance, the best internet security and PC security from cyber security expert, Dr. Leland Benton. As a cyber security expert Dr. Benton performs internet security reviews and cyber security consulting. Protect yourself today!

Judgment Not Included $6.87
Kindle Version
http://www.amazon.com/dp/B00CPRSQ3E
PDF Version
https://www.paypal.com/cgi-bin/webscr?cmd=_s-xclick&hosted_button_id=K9DCZTZ66Y9XL

Crime and Mental Health – Judgment Not Included is all about unbalanced people that commit heinous crimes. It discusses in detail crime and mental health, unbalanced, unbalanced people, mentally ill, mentally disturbed people, mental health issues, and mental disorders as they pertain to crimes committed by unbalanced people. Written by one of the nation's leading behavioral scientists, Dr. Leland

Benton is the author of over two dozen self-help books and nonfiction behavioral science texts. He is a best-selling Amazon author with over 200-books published on Amazon alone. You need to read this book because it teaches you how to protect yourself from unbalanced people as well as why unbalanced people do the things they do. This intriguing book leaves no stone unturned regarding the current events such as the Boston Marathon bombing, the Aurora, Colorado theater shootings, Sandy Hook Elementary School shootings and more.

Protecting Yourself from Cyber Crime $4.87
Kindle Version
http://www.amazon.com/dp/B0095J3EIW
PDF Version
https://www.paypal.com/cgi-bin/webscr?cmd=_s-xclick&hosted_button_id=ANL4P777BCHNQ

Protect Yourself Online – Protecting Yourself From Cyber Crime is all about cyber security online and computer security online. This book shows how to protect yourself and business from online cyber criminals using online computer security programs. Protecting yourself from identity theft and demonstrating various identity protection services as well as credit fraud protection are two of the most common cyber crimes. Protecting Yourself From Cyber Crime is about staying one step ahead of the cyber criminals that are out to steal your life. It only takes one time for it to really hurt! Cyber crime is increasing exponentially and it isn't a matter of if your will be a target; it is simply a matter of when.

But the hunted can become the hunter and fight back. There is an array of free protection software that is easy to install and use and all of the software does a fine job of protecting you and your loved ones. You owe it to yourself to read this book and implement what it teaches. Written by one of the nation's leading cyber forensics investigators and behavioral scientist, Dr. Leland Benton imparts his 31-year expertise to all of his readers. Protect yourself today!

Sleeping with Guns $6.87
Kindle Version
http://www.amazon.com/dp/B00CS1IBZU
PDF Version
https://www.paypal.com/cgi-bin/webscr?cmd=_s-xclick&hosted_button_id=VSZ6KH5YFNK5L

Personal Self Protection – Sleeping with Guns is an epic book that examines the art of self-protection in today's world by examining such topics as guns, guns and crime, guns freedom and terrorism, guns in the workplace, personal protection training, personal protection security, and personal self protection. It delves into touchy topics such as gun control and the mindset of fear. It examines a balanced approach to life where a person can actually enjoy a quality life while still maintaining vigilance against danger.

It provides a variety of alternative forms of protection other than physical weapons such as guns, knives, mace and more. Its main premise is that the human mind is the best defense against any danger or peril. Written by one of the nation's leading behavioral scientist, Dr. Leland Benton examines the science behind the need to protect oneself and loved ones. Dr. Benton is also Chief Forensics Investigator for ForensicsNation and is responsible for over 1100 arrests and conviction of all types of criminals. He is highly qualified to write this book and with over 200-books written on Amazon alone, he is a prolific writer and speaker. This book is a part of his Cyber Crime/Cyber Forensics series of books.

Stealing You $2.99
Kindle Version
http://www.amazon.com/dp/B00778TT6E
PDF Version
https://www.paypal.com/cgi-bin/webscr?cmd=_s-xclick&hosted_button_id=JRW27WXC4H35C

How to Stop Identity Theft – Stealing You not only offers ways to prevent identity theft, it also provides identity theft tips, identity theft resource center, and identity theft help. It also provides information on how to report identity theft correctly and timely. In other words, it is the best desktop compendium on identity theft protection. Everybody knows what identity theft is and there are a plethora of products available that protect against identity theft. But do you know why identity thieves commit this crime and what you do to make their job easier? Now you can crawl inside the heads of identity thieves and see just how vulnerable you are and exactly how you made their job so easy to steal YOU!

SurvivalNations Catalog
Download for Free
http://www.filefactory.com/f/d8ed9a936f3f812e

Are you prepared to survive any disaster or crisis? If the police came to your door and gave you 15-minutes to evacuate, what would you do? Where would you go? What would you take with you? You need SurvivalNations Catalog to answer these questions. We've compiled everything you need to survive in one easy catalog that is at your fingertips. Order SurvivalNations Catalog today!

SurvivalNations – Surviving a Disease Pandemic $6.87
Kindle Version
http://www.amazon.com/dp/B00BFFZCHU
PDF Version
https://www.paypal.com/cgi-bin/webscr?cmd=_s-xclick&hosted_button_id=FJGWFMUJSAENW

SurvivalNations – Surviving a Disease Pandemic is an epic book describing all aspects of an outbreak of a worldwide pandemic and how to protect yourself and loved ones. It is part of Dr. Leland Benton's "Survival Planning series" of books and it describes flu epidemics, what is swine flu, h1n1 virus, what is h1n1, flu outbreak, foodborne disease, and contagious diseases. It is a comprehensive desktop compendium and guidebook that describes everything you need to survive any pandemic.

Survival/Survival Planning
Be A Prepper
http://www.amazon.com/dp/B007IL5OE6

PrepperNations Blueprint
http://www.amazon.com/dp/B00ARBZNCW

Be Prepared to Survive
http://www.amazon.com/dp/B007KJ0ANQ

The Truth About Federal Anti-Hoarding Laws
http://www.amazon.com/dp/B007J4KH4O

Surviving A Financial Crisis $2.99
Kindle Version
http://www.amazon.com/dp/B007J1QH3C
PDF Version
https://www.paypal.com/cgi-bin/webscr?cmd=_s-xclick&hosted_button_id=KTVMQ93UHXDME

Survival Planning – Surviving A Financial Crisis is all about survival preparation, survival information, food for emergency preparedness, supplies for disaster, emergency supplies food, emergency disaster supplies, disaster preparedness kit, and earthquake kits. But more importantly, it is learning how to survive a financial crisis.

It is smart reading and a must read for all family members. It is smart because it is part of a series called "Be Prepared to Survive" and in this series we hope for the best but plan for the worst. Science tells us that only the strong survive. I'm telling you that only the best prepared will survive. Yes, the world economy sucks and it is tough out there but this book will set you on the right path to sound financial planning.

This book provides sound financial guidance even if financial disaster doesn't strike and this author believes it won't. But things will continue to get tougher for at least the next 4-years.

Surviving YOU $2.99
Kindle Version
http://www.amazon.com/dp/B007J3M6A8
PDF Version
https://www.paypal.com/cgi-bin/webscr?cmd=_s-xclick&hosted_button_id=AASNT9YREFQUA

Surviving You is all about leaving your own worst enemy behind – YOU – and becoming your own best friend. We all do things we shouldn't knowing full well that they are either harmful to us or simply plain wrong but we do them anyway. Now you can learn why you do the things you do but more importantly why you don't do the things you should.

The author – Dr. Harry Jay – is one of the leading behavioral scientists in the country and his style of writing makes it easy for you to better understand everything about yourself. But then he takes it a step further and shows you corrective protocols to improve your life. This is a must read book for your personal library.

Get a copy today and soon you will be Surviving YOU!

The Mind Of a Con Man $6.87
Kindle Version
http://www.amazon.com/dp/B00CO2BQHI
PDF Version
https://www.paypal.com/cgi-bin/webscr?cmd=_s-xclick&hosted_button_id=DRUCWHNYDP8F2

Manipulation – The Mind of a Con Man is a book you have ever read before but it is a book you should read! I am going to take you on an adventure into the human mind and show you not only why con men do what they do but why you do the things you do too. It is a unique book describing con man games, con man tricks, con man traits, con man terms, manipulation, emotional manipulator, deception & lies. It is an eye-opening expose taking you into the mind of con men and discovering why they do what they do. This book leaves no stone unturned as it delves deeply into the subject matter. It first describes the Type 1 con men, who are individuals who work hard at the deceptive profession but then it goes even further into Type 2 con men, which you come into contact daily through friends, family, co-workers ,etc that attempt to manipulate you into doing something. This book will fascinate you and you will see yourself within its pages as you learn all about deceptive people, the ways they operate, their tricks, their games and much more. Written by one of the nation's leading behavioral scientists, Dr. Leland Benton is the author of over two dozen self-help books and nonfiction behavioral science texts. He is a best-selling Amazon author with over 200-books published on Amazon alone. You need to read this book.

The Power of Trained Observation $6.87
Kindle Version
http://www.amazon.com/dp/B00BSRYMGW
PDF Version
https://www.paypal.com/cgi-bin/webscr?cmd=_s-xclick&hosted_button_id=QLVW8RH86YW42

Observation Training – The Power of Trained Observation is a series of online observation training courses designed to enhance your leadership skills training and general awareness. You look but you do not see EVERYTHING; you listen but you do not hear. "The Power of Trained Observation" teaches a person how to see EVERYTHING that the eye takes in and how to evaluate it in the conscious mind so the person misses nothing. Learn how the mind filters out stimuli and how to reprogram your filters to take advantage of everything you see and hear using the latest education information technology. Every sales and marketing executive should read this book and take advantage of this brain training online. This book is for anybody in business and investing, marketing and sales, and small business & entrepreneurship. The courses offered are the exact same online police training courses used to train law enforcement. When it comes to observation training, not only is this one of the only courses available, it is the best online training available. Written by one of the nation's leading behavioral scientists and instructors, best-selling author, Dr. Leland Benton is the author of over three dozen books dealing in a variety of behavioral science subjects. He is a best-selling Amazon author with over 200-books published on Amazon alone. If you have a desire to see and hear everything and not miss any opportunities then you need to read this book.

Why Women Should Not Use Online Dating Services $2.99
Kindle Version
http://www.amazon.com/dp/B006J9EMH8
PDF Version
https://www.paypal.com/cgi-bin/webscr?cmd=_s-xclick&hosted_button_id=23GNKD94XL6C2

Cyber Dating Dangers – Why Women Should Not Use Online Dating Sites demonstrates the online dating scams to unsuspecting online singles using singles sites. How online dating is dangerous is described in this book and should be used to understand and spot scam artists so a person can conduct safe online dating. It goes without saying that a person should be careful what online personals they post. Being a woman today is not easy and although the Internet has provided tremendous opportunities, it has also provided criminal elements the very same opportunities to practice their ugly trade. Women that use online dating sites need to read this book!!! You have been warned!

ForensicsNation Catalog
Download for Free Here
http://www.filefactory.com/f/d3eac5e74de46025

Have you been hacked online? Have you had your identity stolen? Have you been receiving weird emails? ForensicsNation Catalog provides you with all the tools to become an amateur sleuth. Be the hunter and not the prey! ForensicsNation Catalog is amateur forensics products enabling you to become an amateur internet sleuth. Cyber-Crime is increasing and now ForensicsNation offers the exact same products it uses to catch the bad guys. Now you can easily find anyone you want and conduct your own investigative searches using the forensic tools we offer.

www.ingramcontent.com/pod-product-compliance
Lightning Source LLC
Chambersburg PA
CBHW071757170526
45167CB00003B/1066